RA

A POCKET GUIDE TO
BIRDS OF PREY & OWLS

Written & Illustrated by

Declan Cairney

To Mathew and
Daniel,

enjoy

ORIGINAL WRITING

ISBN: 978-1-908477-76-7

A CIP catalogue for this book is available from the National Library.

Published by ORIGINAL WRITING LTD., Dublin, 2011.

Printed by CLONDALKIN GROUP, Clonshaugh, Dublin 17

*I dedicate this book to Ben Johnson and
James Irons who were the first to spark
my interest in birds of prey.*

CONTENTS

Foreword

Raptors, a pocket Guide to Birds of Prey and Owls, written and illustrated by Declan Cairney, is a remarkable piece of work. It is the culmination of months of hands-on experience working with raptors in the Burren Birds of Prey Centre, by a birdman who is not yet a teenager! Declan's knowledge and enthusiasm comes through in his writing. His artistic talent is evident in the dramatic poses of his bold illustrations. This pocket guide is thus a handy reference for the many people who, like Declan, admire these noble birds and who look for them both in captive circumstances and in the wild.

Though falcons, hawks and eagles are his first love, Declan has affection for all birds and indeed all nature. Despite his tender years he has, through this book, declared his adult intentions and is clearly well on his way to becoming a fully-fledged naturalist.

Gordon D'Arcy

Declan with Eric the Harris Hawk
at Burren Birds of Prey Centre, Spring 2011
Photograph by Simone Kelly

Introduction

Birds of prey are birds that eat other mammals, birds, fish or insects. Raptor is the name given to a bird of prey that uses its feet to kill. Eagles, hawks, falcons and owls are all raptors. Vultures, along with ravens and carrion crows, are not as they prefer to eat the remains of dead animals. Birds of prey hunt during the day and owls hunt from dusk to dawn.

Throughout the world, many types of bird of prey are endangered. Ireland actually has one of the best environments for birds of prey in Europe but has the least amount. Up until recently we only had six regular breeding types of bird of prey and two types of owl in Ireland but there may once have been 22 regular or occasional breeding raptors. Most bird of prey deaths in Ireland are accidental – the poison bait put out by farmers is intended to kill foxes and crows.

In this book I hope to help people learn about different types of bird of prey, what they look like and where to find them. The name of each bird is given in three formats, English, Latin and Irish (where possible) e.g. **Sparrowhawk – *Accipiter nisus* – Spioróg.** "Sparrowhawk" is the common name, "Accipiter nisus" is the Latin name and "Spioróg" is the name in Irish.

During the summer of 2010 I started to work as a volunteer at Burren Birds of Prey Centre, Ballyvaughan, Co. Clare and I have been helping out there on a regular basis ever since. It is great fun and inspired me to do this book. The proceeds from the sale of this book will be donated to The Golden Eagle Trust Limited.

Burren Birds of Prey Centre,
Aillwee Cave,
Ballyvaughan, Co. Clare
Website: www.birdofpreycentre.com

Golden Eagle Trust Limited,
22 Fitzwilliam Square, Dublin 2
Website: www.goldeneagle.ie

Chapter 1

HAWKS

KILLERS ON THE WING

Although the family name is hawk there are many sub-species; these are kites, buzzards, ospreys and harriers. I have selected five to illustrate and describe. Hawks are expert hunters with extremely powerful feet. The expression "watching you like a hawk" is very good as hawks have supreme eyesight. They circle around the sky. Once prey has been spotted and located they will swoop down and grab it with their *talons*.

Sparrowhawk
Accipiter nisus
Spioróg

The Sparrowhawk is one of the most common birds of prey in Ireland. Although it is small (28-37cm), it is an extremely efficient hunter. In fact, it is quite capable of catching a bird as big as a pheasant although this is quite rare. Sparrowhawks usually hunt by snatching small, unwary birds out of the sky. As their name suggests, they hunt sparrows but also other birds and small mammals. However, Sparrowhawks are prey themselves as larger birds of prey such as buzzards can hunt them. Sparrowhawks can often be found in woodland areas because they are very good at **tail-chasing** and are very **agile**. The Sparrowhawks natural habitat (woodland areas) provides some protection for the Sparrowhawk from larger birds which don't have their agility.

Harris Hawk
Parabuteo unicinctus

The Harris Hawk is not any normal hawk. Most hawks are *solitary* predators and will only come together during *breeding*, but not the Harris Hawk. It is the world's only *social raptor* and a lot of the time hunts in packs. This also makes it one of the most efficient hunters on the planet. They have been seen standing one on top of the other to obtain a better view of the landscape. They are residents of the southern states of the USA down through Central and South America. However, there are Harris Hawks in Ireland because they are popular birds for *falconers* to keep due to their *social* nature.

Red Kite
Milvus milvus
Cúr

The red kite is a beautiful bird with reddish brown colouration and a deeply forked tail. It is often seen soaring very high in the sky. Kites are quite large birds with fully grown females having a wingspan of up to 1.9m. Red Kites used to be very common in Ireland and thanks to re-introduction programs in Co. Wicklow and North Co. Dublin, they should be again. They are extremely adaptable and will eat almost anything, so they will not only live in the countryside but will hopefully adapt to living near *urban* areas as well.

Despite their size Red Kites are actually quite weak. The largest animal a Red Kite could kill is a rabbit.

Common Buzzard
Buteo buteo
Clamhán

The Common Buzzard is a medium sized *raptor* (50-57cm) and can often be seen in Ireland sitting in trees and on fences along major road-sides. This is because of the availability of *carrion* in the form of *road-kill* (buzzards, like all birds of prey are lazy!). They also eat earthworms, but in winter when the ground is frozen, they can catch and eat animals as big as rabbits. They are quite an impressive sight as they are large and bulky creatures.

The Rough-legged Buzzard - *Buteo lagopus*
Clamhán lópach (also shown) is slightly larger but a rare visitor to Ireland from Scandinavia.

Goshawk
Accipiter gentilis
Seabhac

The Goshawk can easily be confused with a Sparrowhawk as they are almost identical in shape - the Goshawk is slightly different in colour and much larger in size. Goshawks are very rare in Ireland but if you are lucky and you see one it will be an impressive sight. An adult female can have a wing span of around 1.6m and as usual with birds of prey she is much larger than the male. Goshawks have bright yellow legs and eyes with a stripe above them, when they are flying you can see that for the most part their underside is white. Goshawks are powerful birds and can catch things up to the size of a Pheasant.

Osprey
Pandion hailaetus
Iascaire Coirneach

The Osprey is an unusual bird of prey because it feeds only on fish. It does this by eyeing the water either while flying or sitting in a tree. Once prey has been spotted the Osprey swoops in and plunges into the water often submerging completely. If the fish is caught it is usually carried head first to reduce wind drag. Ospreys have a black eye stripe that tells them apart from other *raptors*. Their blue-grey feet are equipped with special pads to help grip slippery fish.

Chapter 2

OWLS

TWILIGHT ASSASSINS

Most owls hunt at **dawn** and **dusk,** although many people think they are all **nocturnal**. They have extremely good long-distance eyesight but like all **raptors**, they have no sense of smell. Their primary sense is hearing. Their disk shaped face catches sound and pushes it back to their ears which are off-set (one higher than the other). They can turn their head three quarters of the way round. There are numerous species of owl, from the tiny Burrowing Owl (22cm high) to the massive Eagle Owl (75cm high). I have just chosen four to illustrate for this book.

Barn Owl
Tyto alba
Scréachóg Reilige

The Barn Owl used to be one of the most common owls in Ireland but it is in decline because of changes in farming practices. It can be seen hunting on open farm land or moor land. As its name suggests it often nests in barns when it has young. Adult Barn Owls have a beautiful, white, heart-shaped face and yellow body, if you get a close enough look you may see the white and black dots on its plumage. It might come as a surprise to you that owls are more closely related to the Cuckoo and Nightjar than they are to other birds of prey.

Long-eared Owl
Asio otus
Ceann Cait

The Long-eared Owl is probably the most unusual bird of prey in Ireland. With its tall, thin body and abnormally large ear tufts it is a freakish sight. This type of owl is a lovely chocolate brown colour with black speckles and it has an orange face. Despite the name "Long-eared Owl", the ear tufts on the top of its head are not its ears. Its ears are on each side of its head, behind its eyes. They are offset which gives them extremely good hearing!

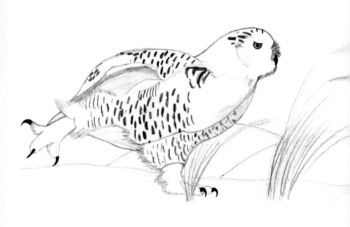

Snowy Owl
Babo scandiaca
Ulcabhán Sneachtúil

The Snowy Owl is one of the top predators on the Arctic Tundra (the vast plane that covers most of northern Canada, Greenland and Russia). Being one of the few *raptors* hunting on the Tundra it has little competition. The male owls have a snow white colour overall (hence the name snowy owl), however the females have dark brown speckles. Probably the most striking thing about the Snowy Owl is its large hypnotic yellow eyes which like all owls don't move in their sockets.

European Eagle Owl
Bubo bubo
Uallchabhán

The European Eagle Owl is in-fact the largest owl in the world. It gets the name "eagle owl" because it is so big, like an eagle. The European Eagle Owl is not the only eagle owl in the world - there are others such as the Ethiopian Eagle Owl. As its name suggests the European Eagle Owl lives in most of main land Europe but it can also be found in northern Asia (hence its other name, the Eurasian Eagle Owl).

Chapter 3

EAGLES

KINGS OF THE SKY

Eagles are the largest type of *raptor* in the world. The biggest type of eagle in the world is the Steller's Sea Eagle of northern Russia. Eagles are powerful high flyers and because of this they have often been used as a symbol of power and sometimes war. Like all birds of prey eagles have no sense of smell so they rely on sight to hunt. If you were to go looking for eagles, coastal or mountainous areas would be the best places to look. This is because eagles such as the Golden Eagle like to hunt mountain hares and eagles such as the Bald Eagle like to hunt fish. In Ireland the Golden Eagle Trust Limited have re-introduced Golden Eagles and White-tailed Sea Eagles.

Golden Eagle
Aquila chrysaetos
Iolar Fírean

The Golden Eagle, along with its close cousin the White-tailed Sea Eagle, is one of the most widespread eagles in the world. It is found throughout Europe and northern parts of Asia and America. This type of eagle is quite large, growing up to 91cm in height with a wingspan of up to 2.2 m. However, it is not as big as the White-tailed Sea Eagle. Golden Eagles tend to be built like hawks and they have long tails. White-tailed Sea Eagles on the other hand have short tails and are built more like vultures. Golden Eagles are rare in Ireland as they have fallen victim to poisoned baits like many other birds such as Red Kites and White-tailed Sea Eagles.

White-tailed Sea Eagle
Haliaeetus albicilla
Iolar Mara

The White-tailed Sea Eagle (also known as the White-tailed Eagle) is the largest bird of prey on the western side of Europe. It can grow to be up to 77cm long with a wing span of 2.45m. Although Golden Eagles have a longer body, White tailed Sea Eagles are classified as larger because the have a larger wing span and a more muscular body. White-tailed Sea Eagles are in fact just like North American Bald Eagles but in Europe their head is not pure white. As its name suggests the White-tailed Sea Eagle likes to live and hunt near the sea. It sits somewhere high and when it sees a large fish below the surface of the water it will swoop down and grab it in its powerful feet, piercing the fish with its *talons*. The White tailed Eagle is now the national symbol of Poland.

Bald Eagle
Haliaeetus leucocephalus
Iolar Maol

The Bald Eagle is probably one of the most famous birds of prey in the world. One of the factors that make it so famous is that it is the national symbol of America. Another factor could be its beautiful colouration. Bald Eagles are the second largest birds of prey in America and can have a wing span of 2.5m. Because of their size they need an extremely large nest and biologists in Alaska found Bald Eagle nests that were 3m across and weighed 2 tonnes. Bald Eagles were given the term "bald" because of their beautiful white heads which makes the huge beak stand out. But it is not their huge beaks that are their most dangerous weapon - like all **raptors** it is their feet that they use to catch and kill their prey. Bald Eagles have an aggressive nature and often steal food from each other and sometimes even fight while flying.

Steller's Sea Eagle
Haliaeetus pelagicus

Named after the German botanist, George Steller, the world's largest eagle the Steller's Sea Eagle has made its home in Russia and northern Europe. However it has been spotted in Alaska and northern Canada and hopefully will make its home there too. The Steller's Sea Eagle is a truly gigantic bird with a wingspan of up to 2.5m. They are classified as *vulnerable* with an estimated *population* of 5,000 specimens. With size comes power and a fully grown Steller's Sea Eagle is indeed a very powerful bird.

Harpy Eagle
Harpia harpyja

Harpy Eagles are the second largest *raptors* in the world. They have the largest and most powerful feet for their size. They also have the longest *talons* of any bird of prey in the world. Unlike other large eagles, such as the Steller's Sea Eagle, the Harpy Eagle has agility making it the ultimate bird of prey. They need their agility to help them catch prey such as monkeys, sloths and some large females can even catch tapirs (pig-sized mammals with a small trunk-like nose). They are residents of the jungles of South America. Harpy Eagles can easily be identified by the distinctive crest of feathers which they sport on their head.

Chapter 4

VULTURES

AND OTHER SCAVENGERS

Vultures and their relatives are unlike any other bird of prey. This is because they do not hunt. Instead they are scavengers - watchers of the dead. Many species are found in Africa and Asia. They are true high flyers – the highest flying bird in the world being the Griffon Vulture which has been seen flying at an *altitude* of 3000ft. Ravens are not in the vulture family but are the largest of the crow family. They, like vultures and condors, mostly scavenge for food and this is why I have included them here.

African White-Backed Vulture
Gyps africanus
Bultúr Bán-tacaíocht na hAfraice

The African White-backed Vulture (close cousin of the Asian White-backed Vulture) is a typical vulture. They do not hunt but instead they sit in trees around a lion or hyena kill and wait until the larger predators have had their fill, then they swoop down and scoff up all the leftovers. African White-backed Vultures can fly at 2000ft - this is because the higher they go the more land they can *survey.*

Condor
Vultur gryphus

The condor is the largest bird of prey in the world with fully grown females having a wing span of up to 3m. All species of Condor scavenge for food. The Condor is so big in fact that it can't take to the air without the help of rising air currents, but when it is in full swing it is a master of flight and aerial motion. Some Condor's have been known to fly at heights of over 2000 ft surveying their territory. They are resident in the southern parts of the USA as well as through Central and South America.

The Common Raven
Corvus corax
Fiach Dubh

The Raven is the largest, most powerful and intelligent of all the crow family. Looking like a large crow it can catch things like rats, mice, small birds and even young rabbits, but most of the time it scavenges for food. The nest of a Raven is a massive structure of sticks - the inside is lined with sheep's wool, rabbit fur, etc. The Raven has beautiful blush green eggs with dark brown to black speckles. The **clutch** varies from three to seven eggs. The Raven's nest is sometimes taken over by Peregrines and pairs of them have been seen enduring aerial battles.

Chapter 5

FALCONS

BIRDS OF SPORT

Falcons stand out from other birds of prey for one reason in particular - their speed. Although they are among the smallest birds of prey in the world, they are also among the fastest living creatures in the world. The first birds to be used by man to hunt were the Saker Falcons of Asia. They were used during harsh winters to hunt for food for the villagers and were released in spring when food became more readily available. Nowadays, all over the world, trained, licensed, *falconers* keep falcons for sport and use them to hunt on approved lands.

The Peregrine Falcon
Falco peregrinus
Fabhcún Gorm

The Peregrine is in fact the fastest living thing known to man. A wild female was clocked at nearly 250 mph (400kph). Peregrines hunt by finding **thermals** and soaring high into the air. Once prey has been located below the Peregrine will close its wings and dive at an astronomical speed – this is what peregrines are renowned for, the so called "*stoop*". The sheer force of the Peregrines *stoop* is what kills its prey instantly. The Peregrine has extremely large feet for its body size which makes walking quite awkward so you will never see one of these birds travel far on foot.

Lanner Falcon
Falco biarmicus

The Lanner Falcon is a small speedy bird of prey that hunts in much the same way as a Peregrine. It lives in southern parts of Europe such as Spain, Italy and all of Africa. The Lanner Falcon feeds mainly on small to medium-sized birds, ranging from larks up to ducks and guinea fowl and sometimes even other falcons. Small mammals such as rodents and bats may also be taken along with insects and spiders. It is known that sometimes up to 20 Lanner Falcons may gather to feed at places like colonial nesting sights or grass fires where prey is plentiful.

Kestrel
Falco tinnunculus
Pocaire Gaoithe

The Kestrel is Ireland's most common and familiar bird of prey. It can often be seen hovering in the air above a roadside or at a cliff-edge scanning the ground below for signs of prey. It usually catches small rodents such as shrews and mice but in the summer months will also catch large insects such as beetles. The male plumage on its back and the tops of its wings is a distinctive chestnut brown with black spots. The female Kestrel (shown here) is however a much darker and duller colour brown.

Hobby
Falco subbuteo
Fabhcún Coille

The Hobby may be small and slim, but it is fast and nimble in the air. Ireland is just off the migration path for these birds but occasionally they stop along the southern coast in springtime. They hunt prey such as dragonflies and mayflies but in summer they can catch birds such as Swallows, Martins and Swifts. When close up, they seem to be wearing a pair of bright red trousers, but this is really just their leg feathers. The Hobby is the second smallest bird of prey found in Ireland (the smallest is the Merlin).

Gyrfalcon
Falco rusticolus
Fabhcún Mór

The Gyrfalcon is actually the biggest falcon on earth. A fully grown female can have a wingspan of up to 1.6m - that is the size of a male Buzzard! The Gyrfalcon's success in hunting usually comes from its strength and size. When hunting, they don't always *stoop* on prey like most other falcons - instead they hunt by launching out of a hiding place and *tail-chasing* their prey like a hawk. Gyrfalcons can come in three different phases of colour. The dark phase (shown here) is mainly found in Scandinavia, the white phase is mainly found in Greenland and the grey phase is mostly found in Iceland but also Greenland and Scandinavia. The Gyrfalcon's diet mainly consists of large game birds such as pheasant, grouse and partridge but it will also take mammals such as rabbits and hares.

Glossary of Terms

Agile   Fast and able to turn quickly at high speeds

Altitude   Height above sea level

Breeding   Animals coming together to have young

Carrion   Flesh of dead animals

Clutch   Group of eggs laid by a bird

Dawn   Morning time/sunrise

Dusk   Evening time/sunset

Falconer   A person who keeps falcons and hawks for sport

Nocturnal   Animals and birds that are most active at night time

Population   The number of a particular animal living in the wild

Raptor   Bird that uses its feet to kill its prey

Road-kill	Animals and birds killed by passing traffic
Social	Living in groups
Solitary	Living and hunting alone, not in groups
Stoop	High speed diving attack
Survey	To look over an area
Tail-chasing	Chasing something directly from behind, only a tail length away
Talons	The claws on a bird of preys' feet
Thermal	Warm column of rising air
Urban	In towns and cities or built up areas
Vulnerable	Exposed to danger

Bibliography

Birds of Britain And Europe
Volker Dierschke
A&C Black Publishers Ltd. 2008

Birds of Prey Colouring Book
John Green
Dover Publications Inc. 1989

Encyclopedia of Birds
Edited by Christopher Perrins
Oxford University Press 2009

Guinness World Records 2010
Guinness World Records Ltd. 2009

Intelligence In Animals
Reader's Digest 1995

Irish Birds their Nests and Eggs
Críostóir Ó Deargáin
Carraig Print Ltd 2010

The Complete Guide To Ireland's Birds
Eric Dempsey & Michael O'Clery
Gill & Macmillan Ltd 2002

Untamed
Steve Bloom
Harry N. Abrams Inc. 2008

World of Science
Miles Kelly
Miles Kelly Publishing 2006

Acknowledgements

I would like to thank the following people, without whose help this book would not have been possible:

Gordon D'Arcy
Clare Horan & Gerry Wallace
Bríd Horan
James Irons
Ben Johnson
Simone Kelly
Lorcán O'Toole
The staff and volunteers at Burren Birds of Prey Centre
My parents, Hugh & Maeve, and my younger brother Ruarí